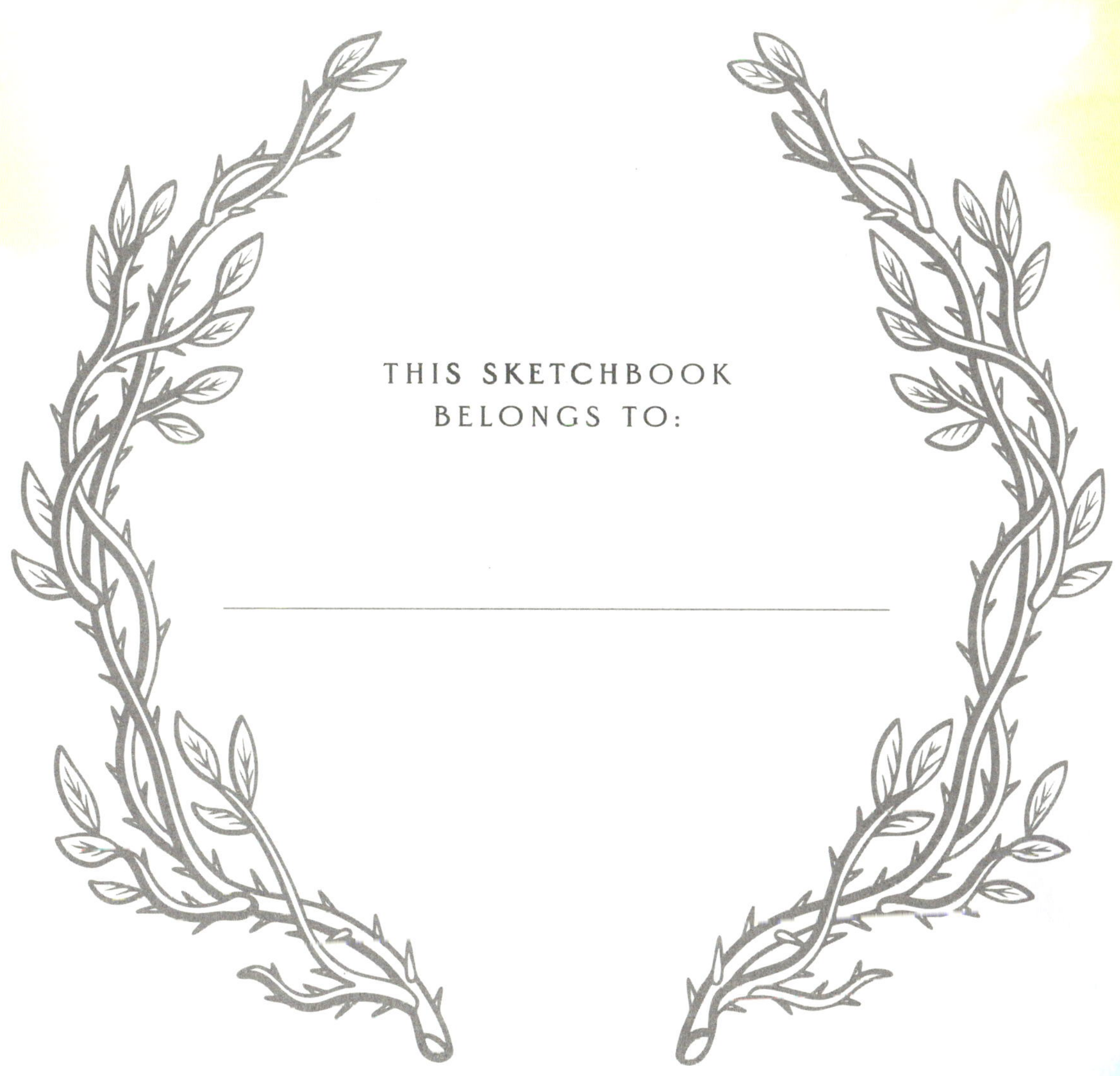

weldon**owen**

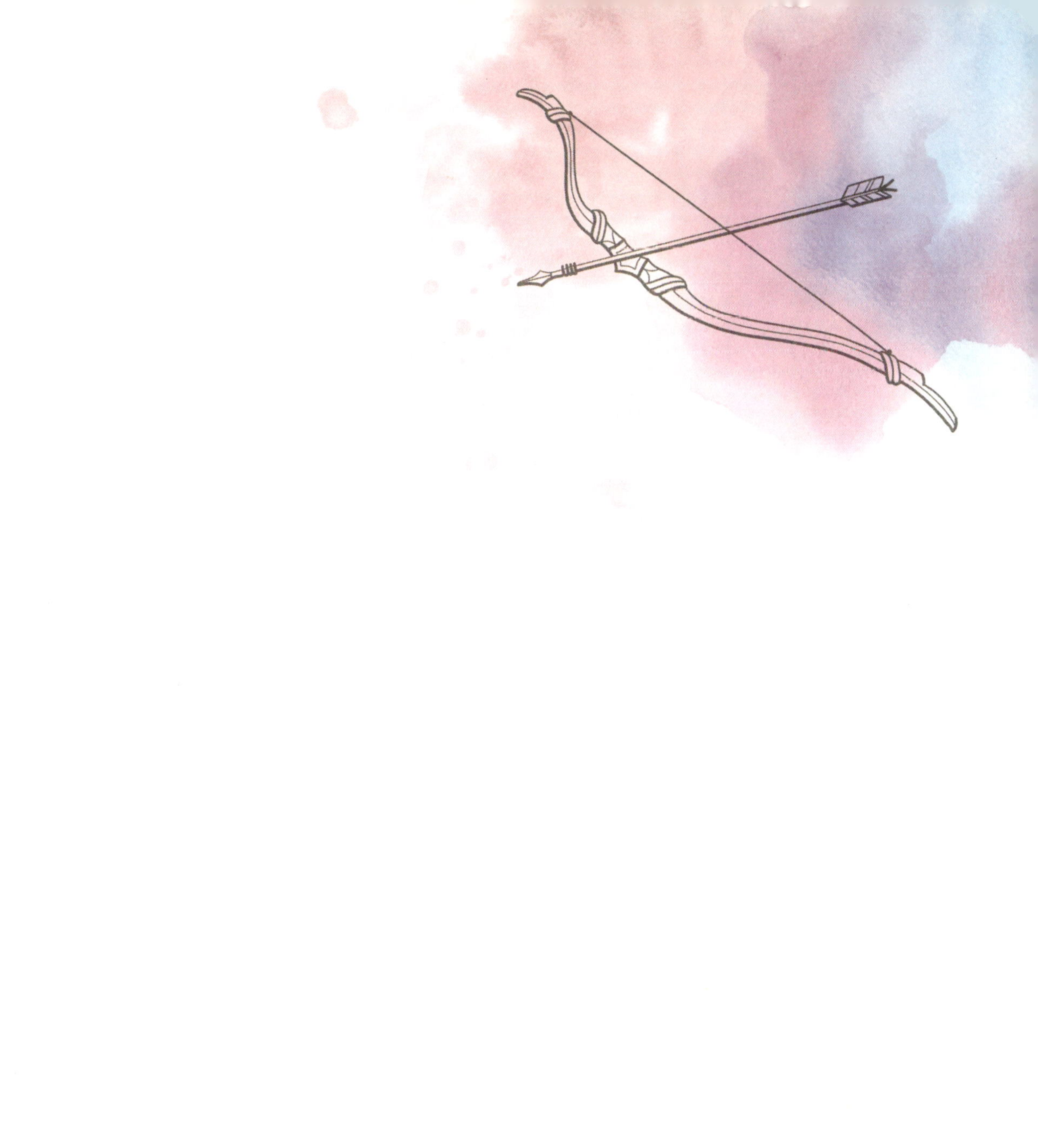

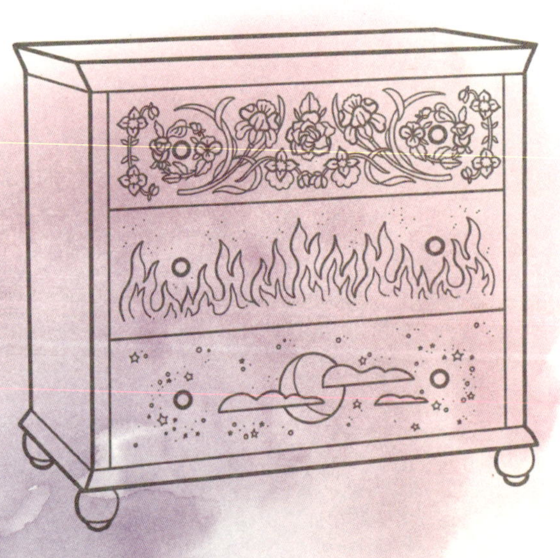

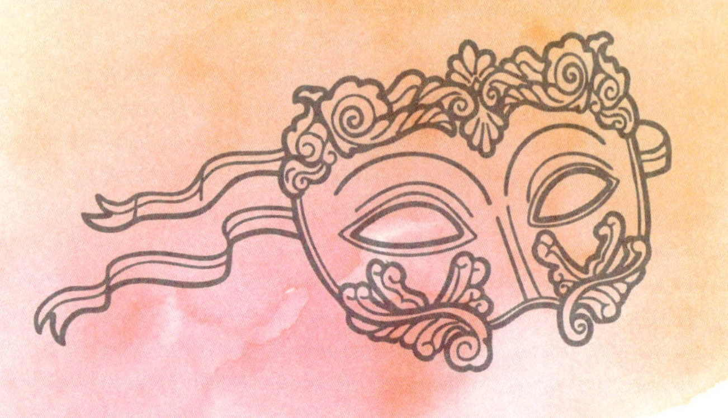

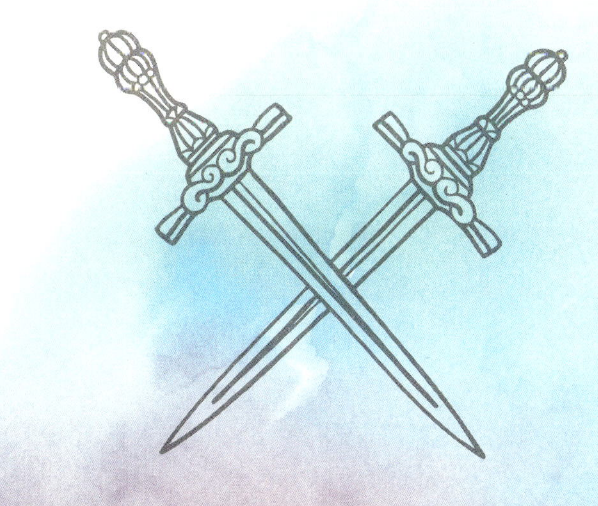

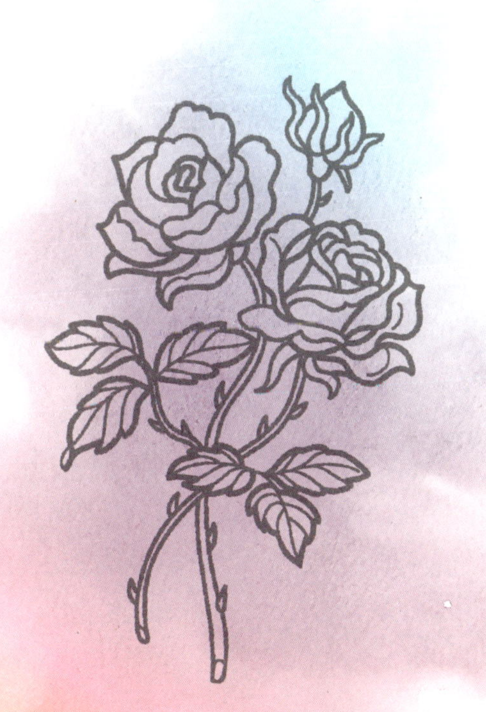

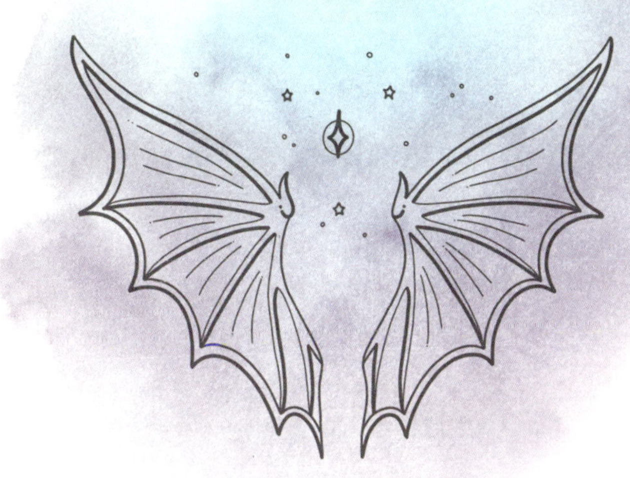

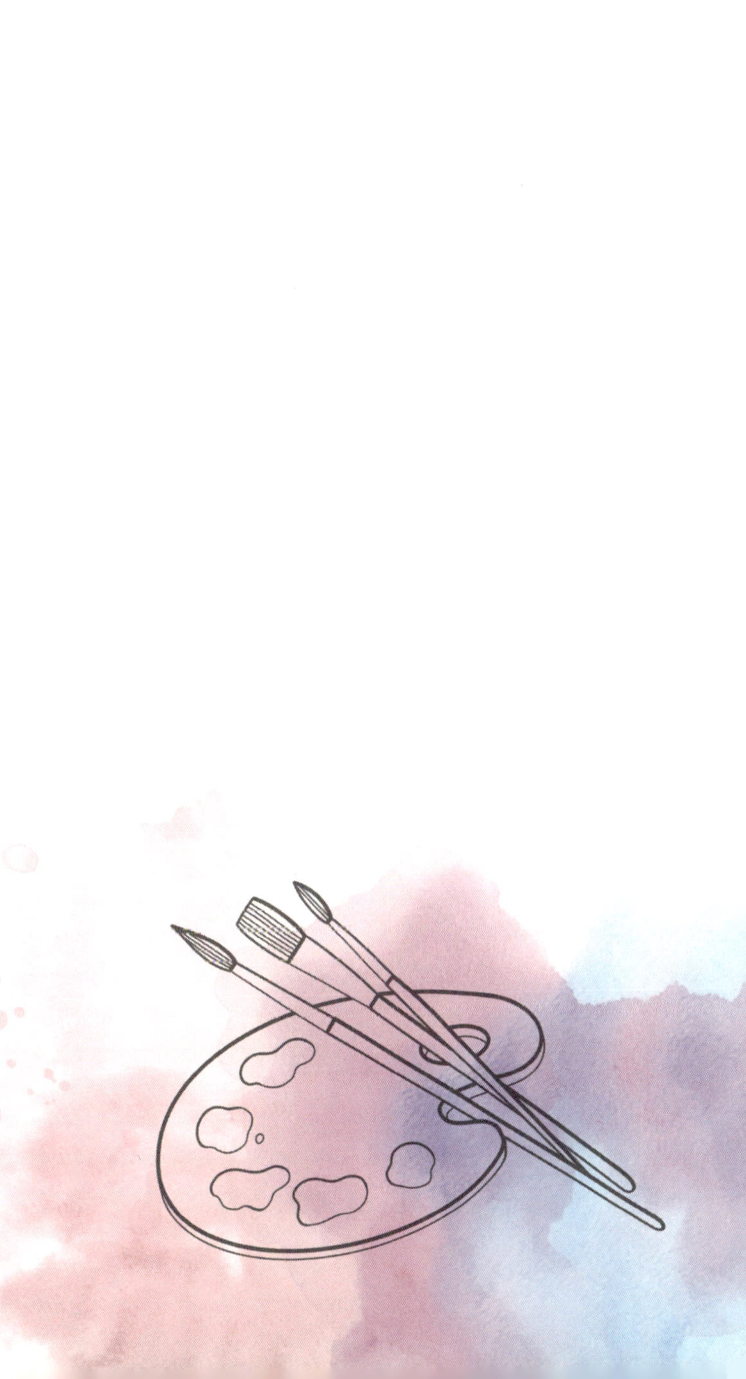

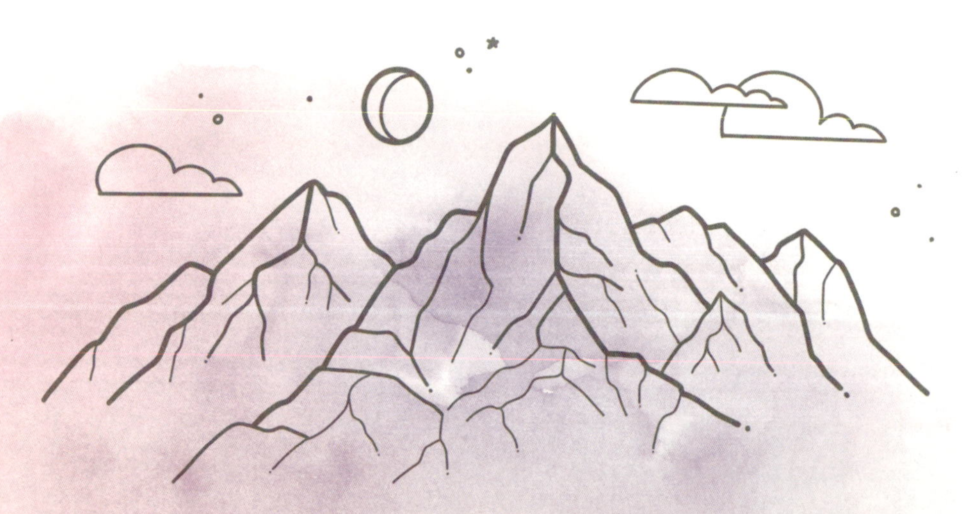

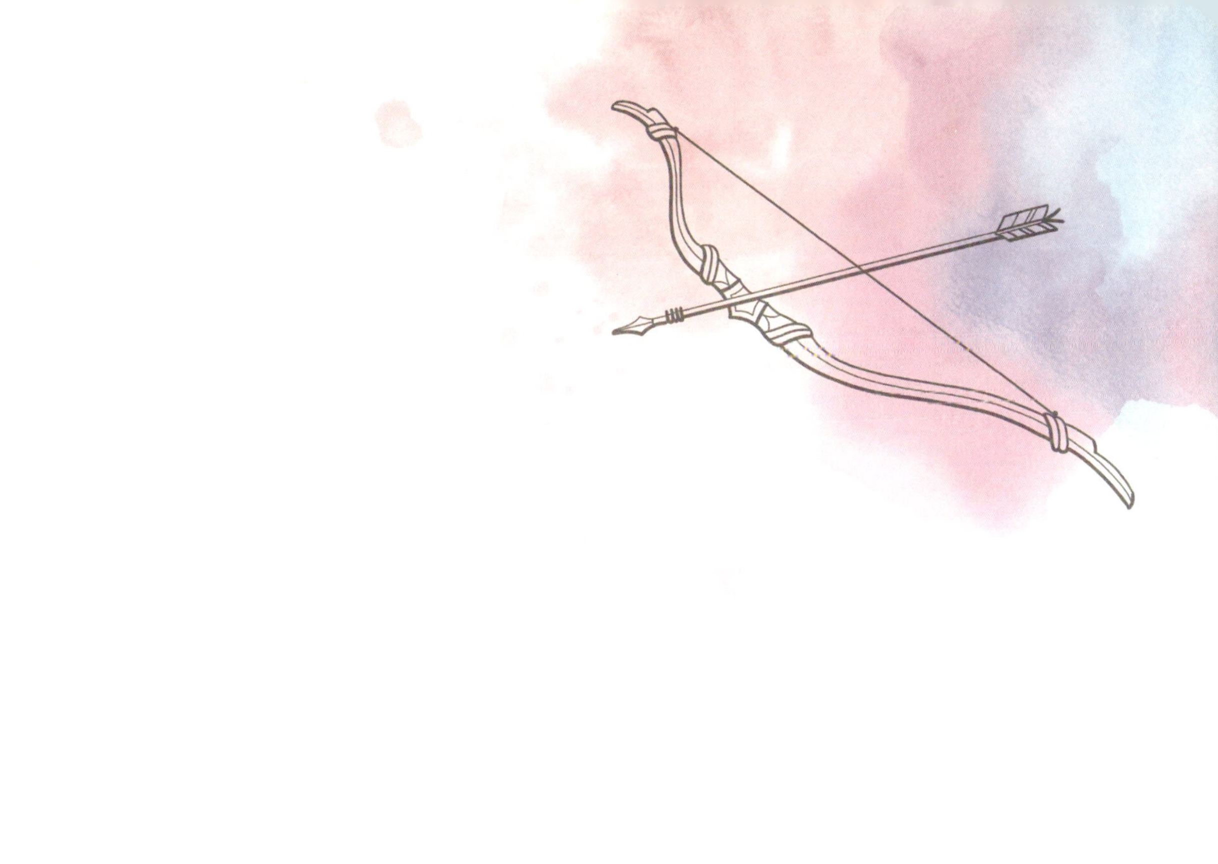

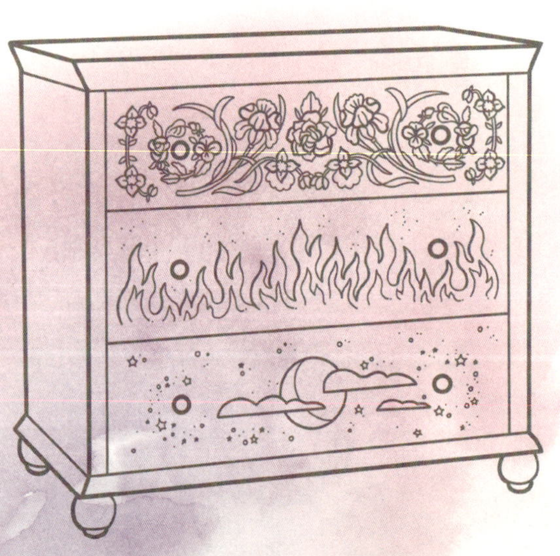

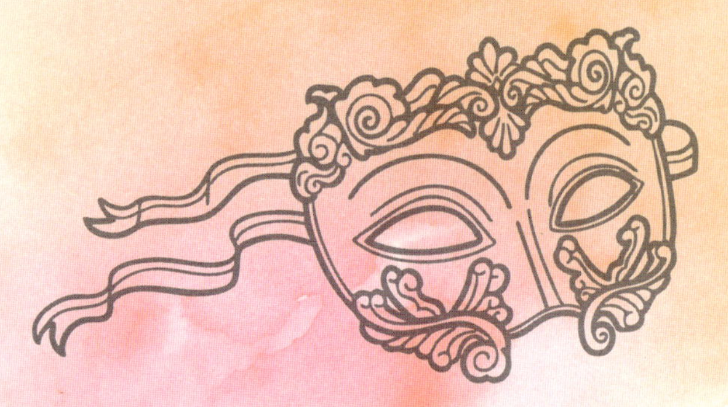

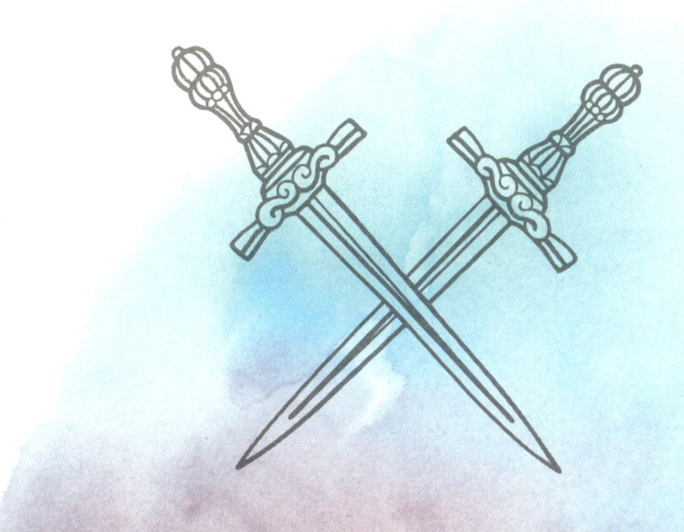

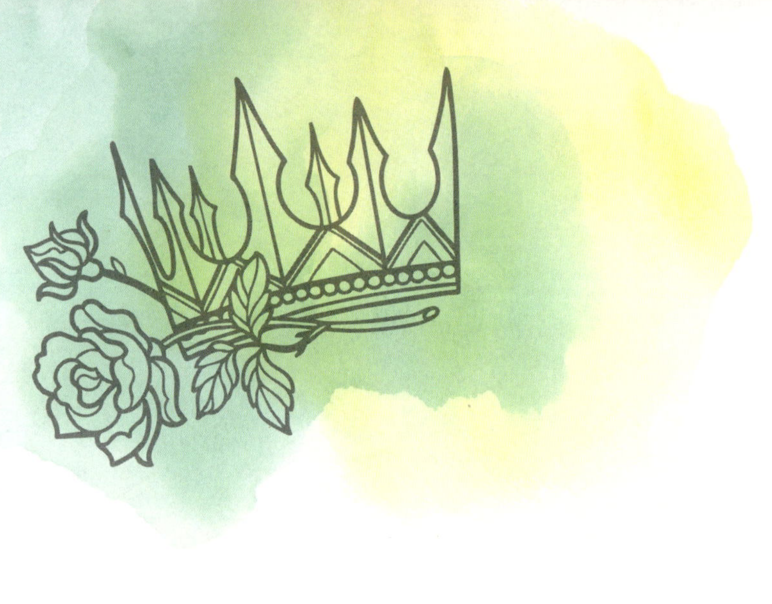

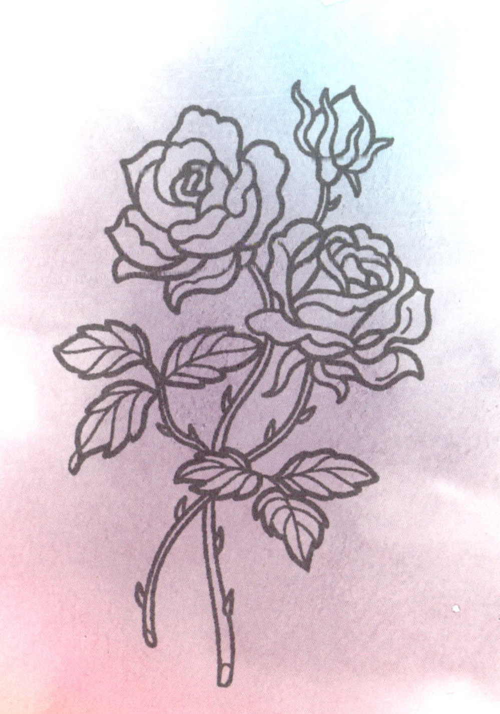

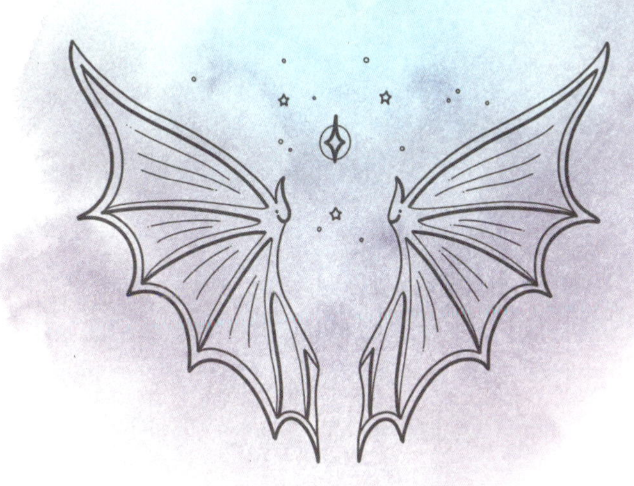

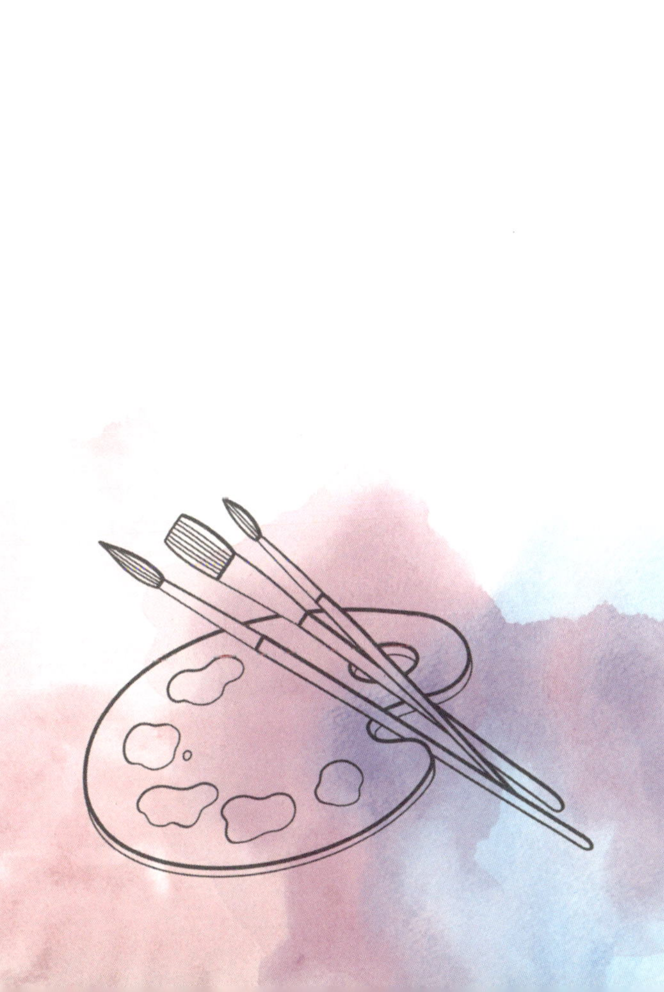

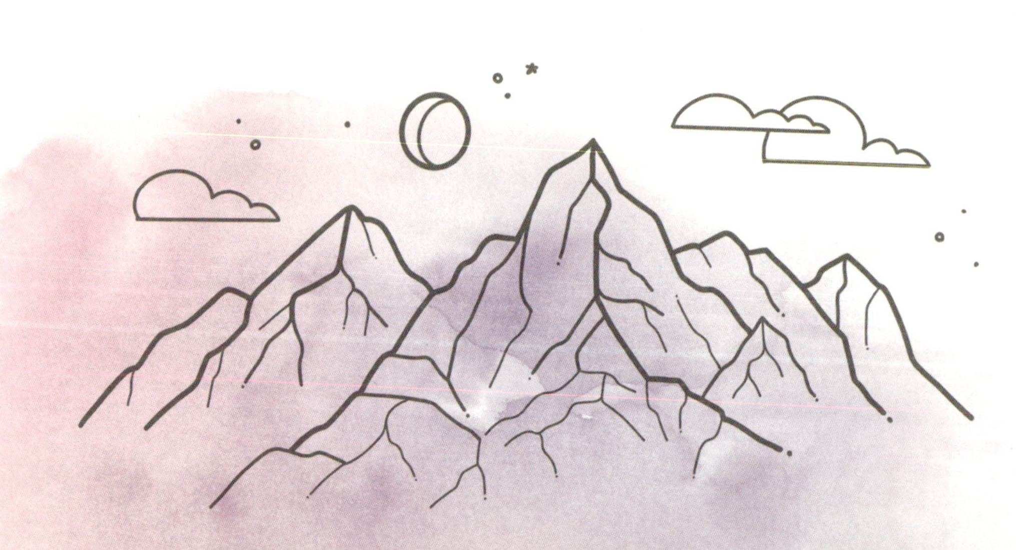

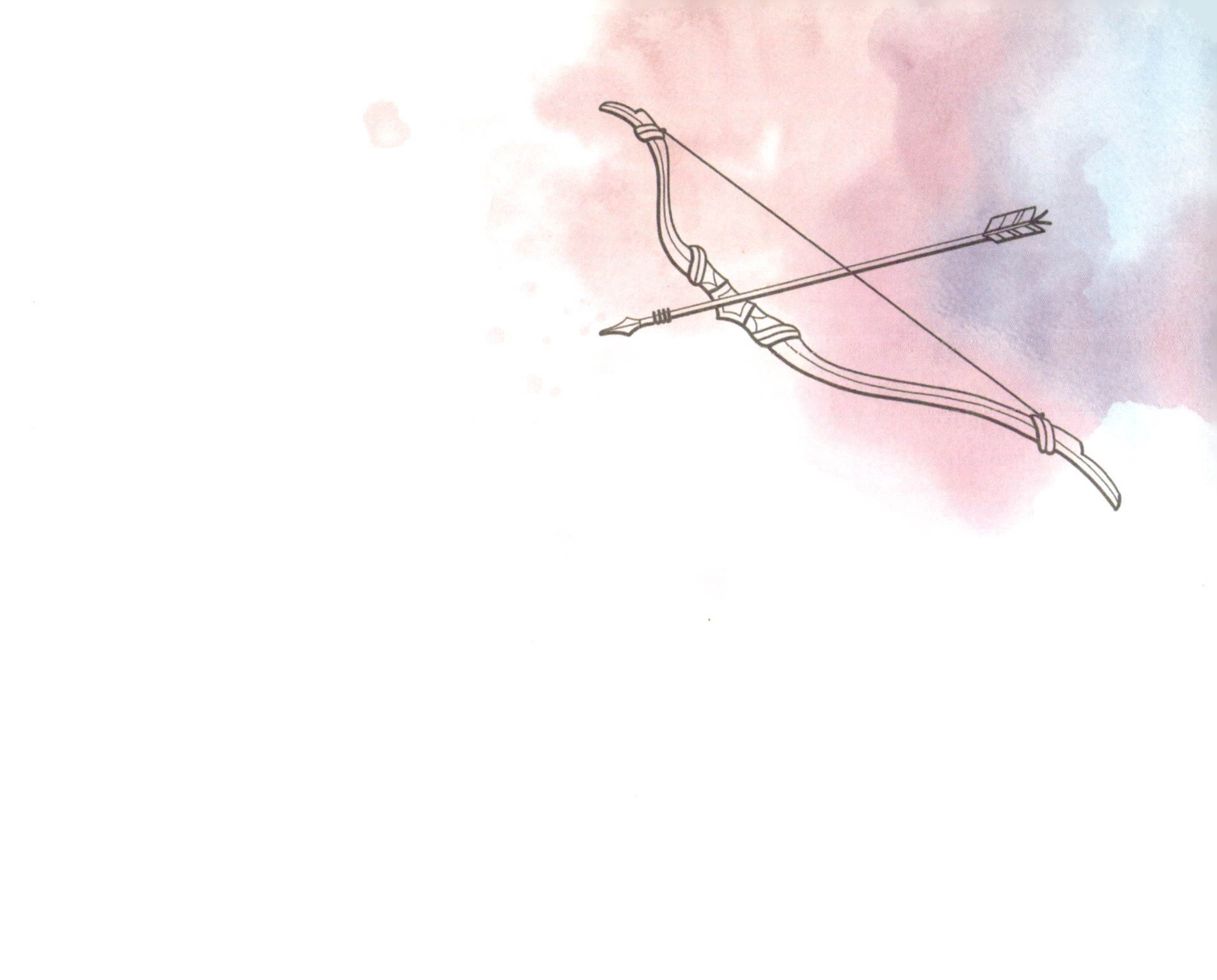

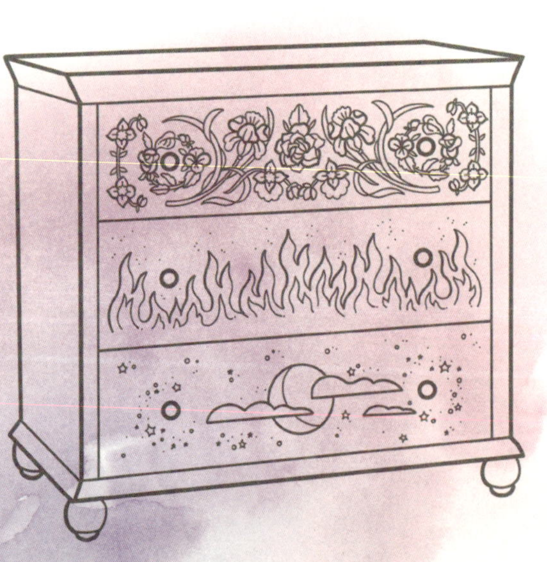

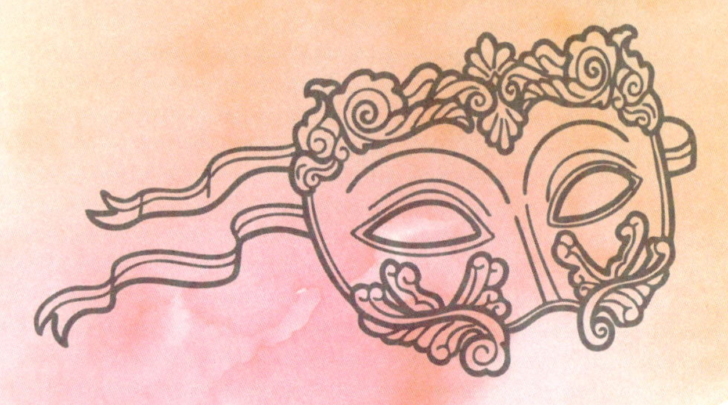

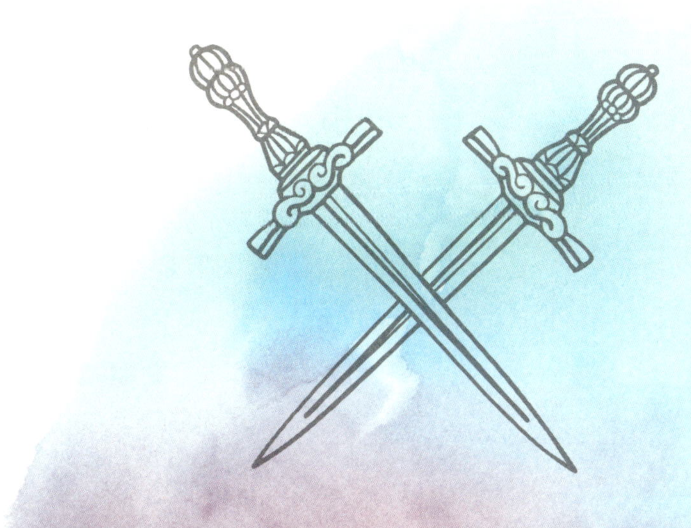

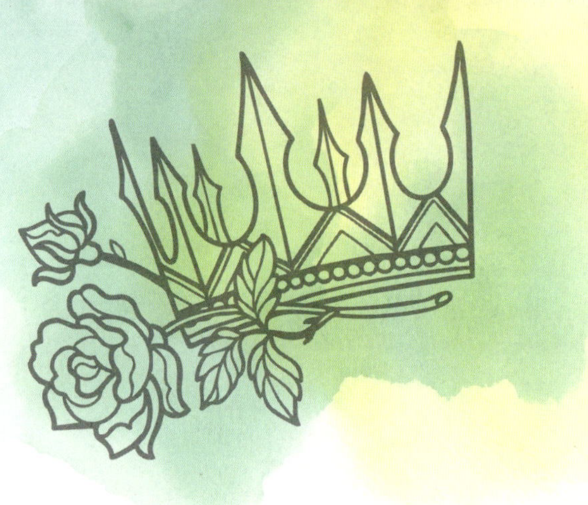

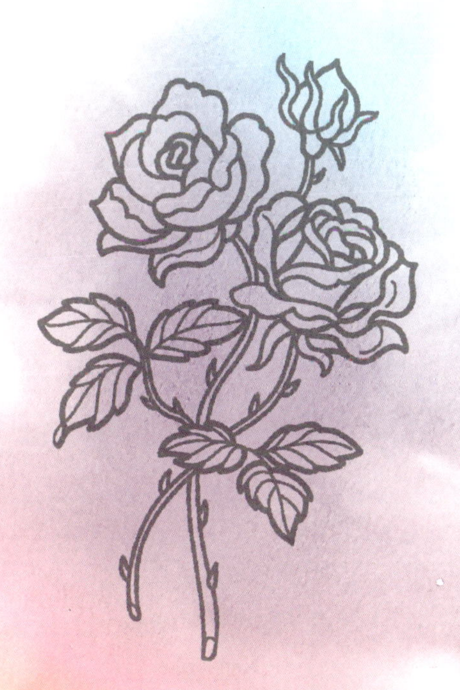

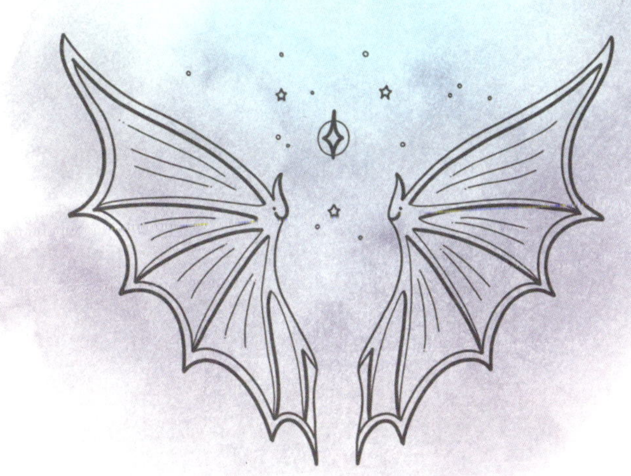

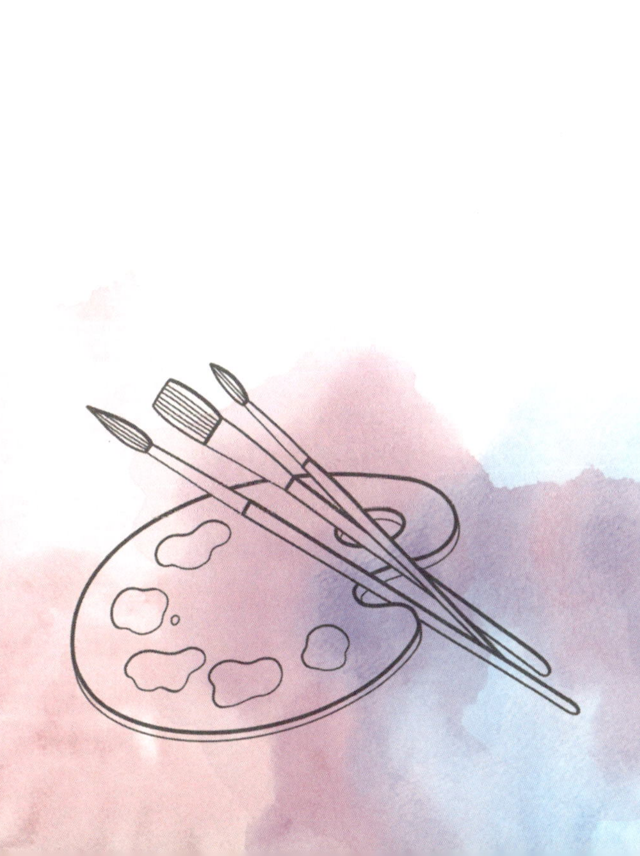

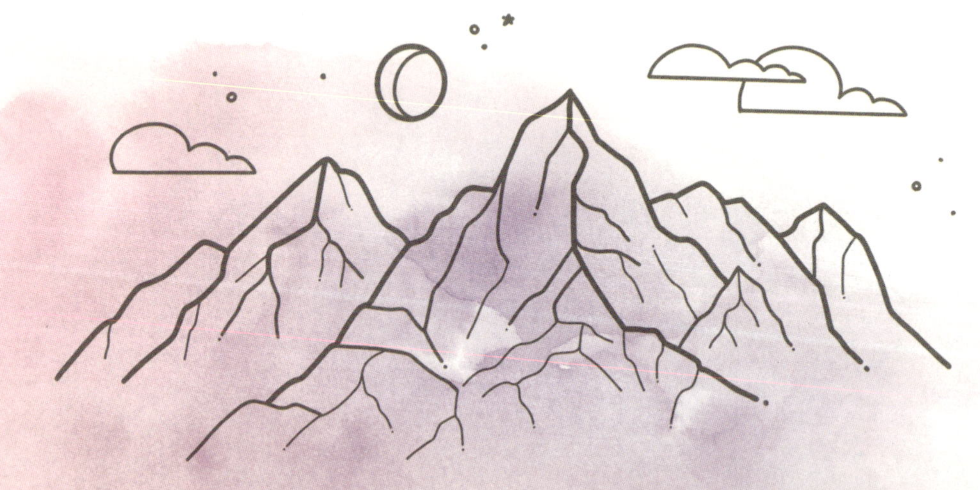

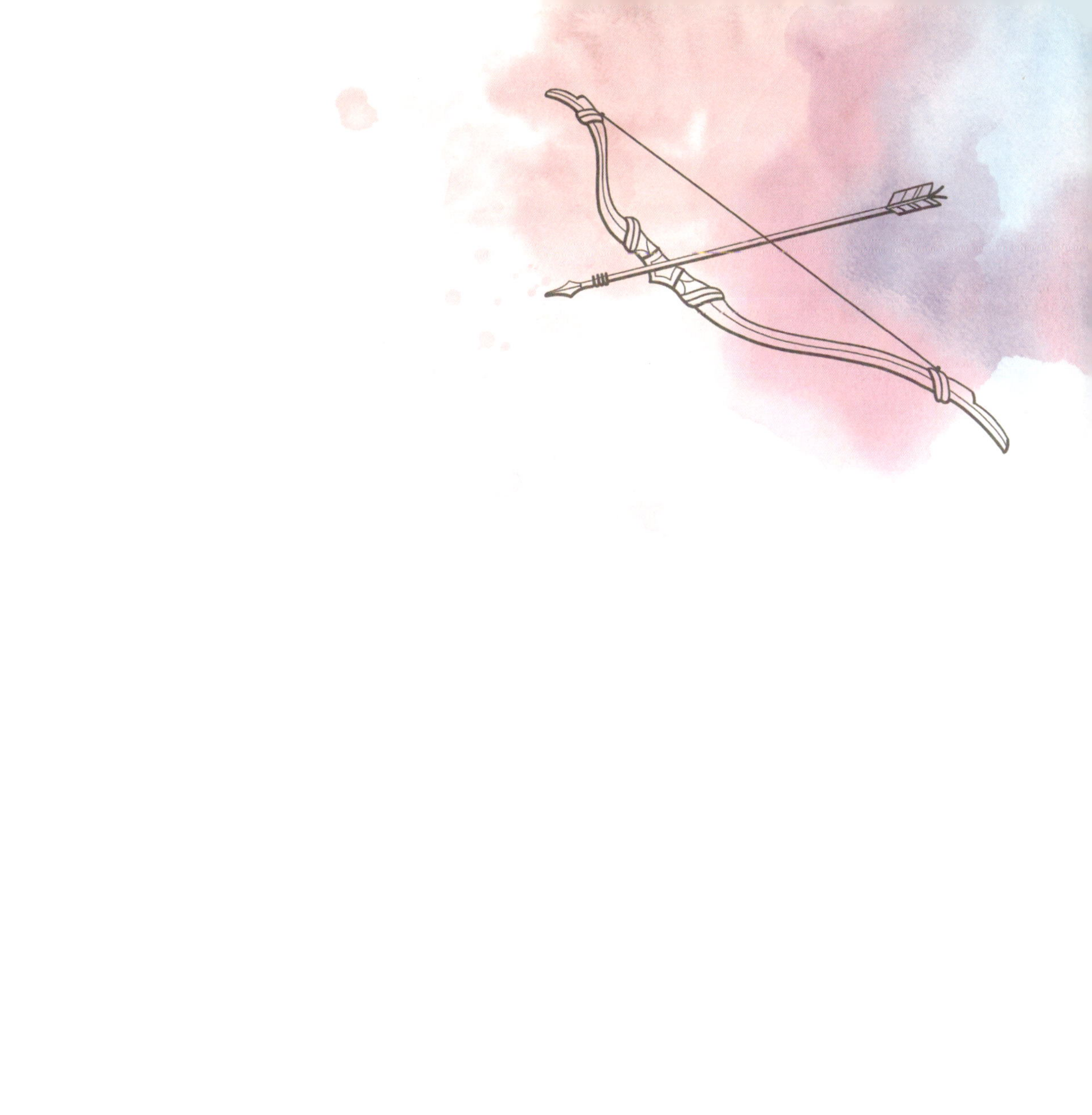

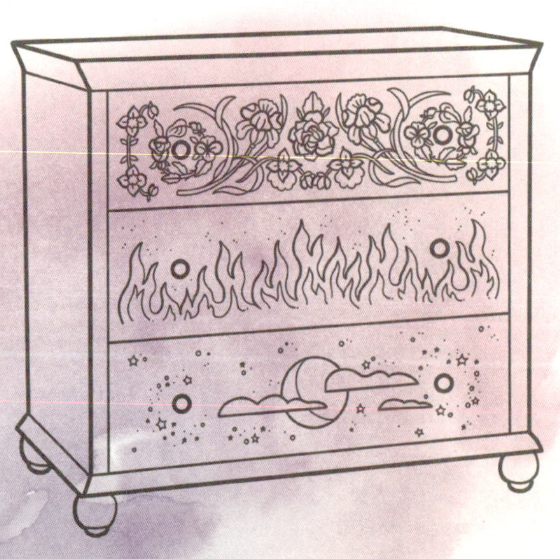

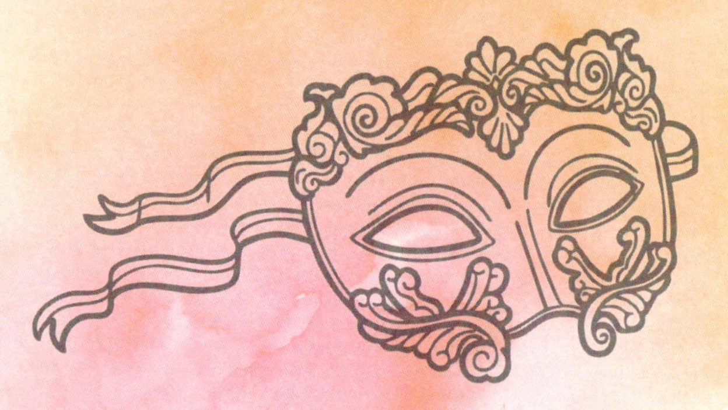

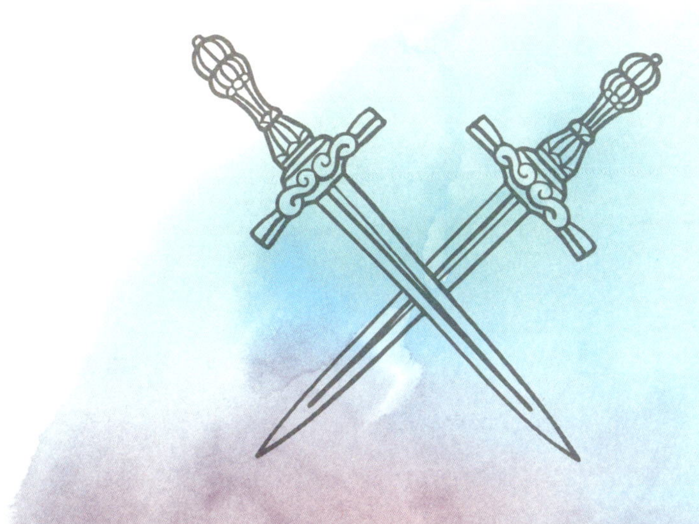

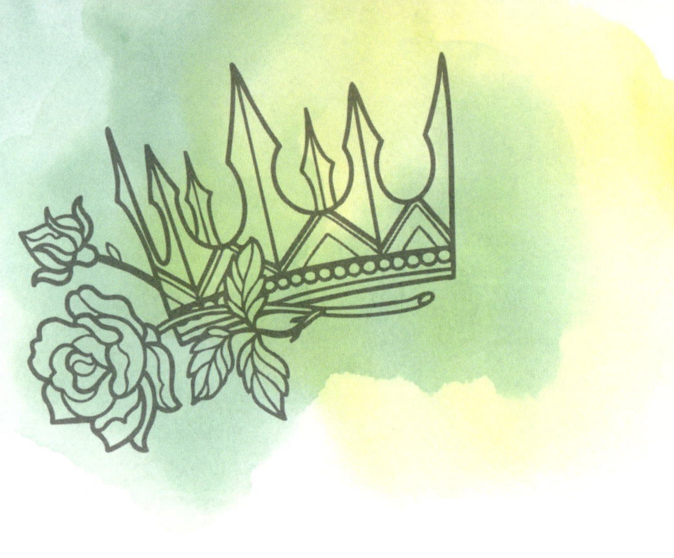

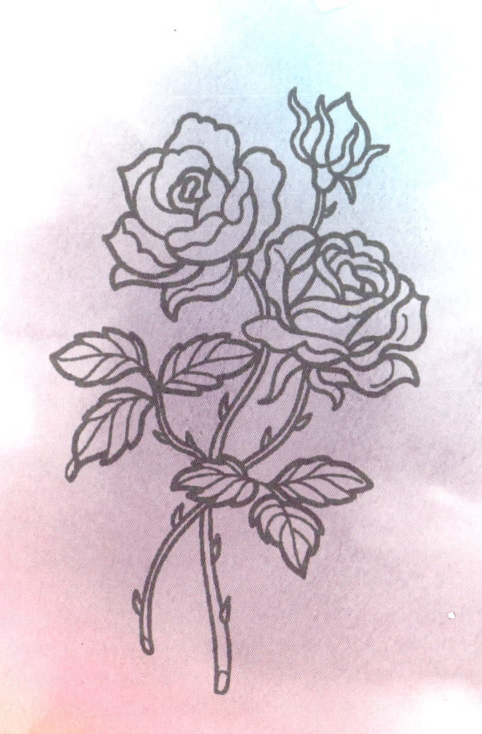

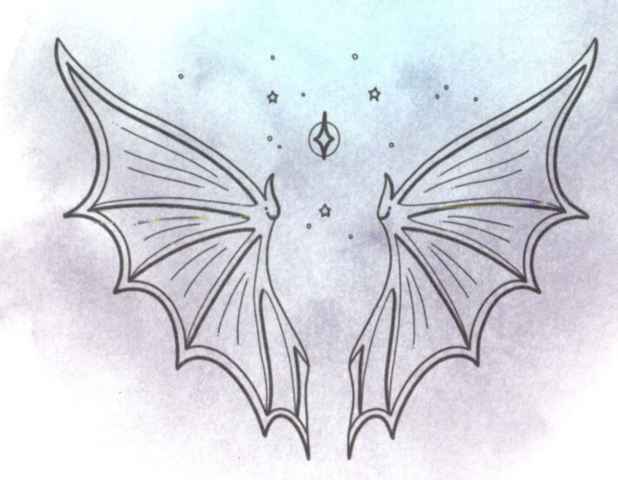

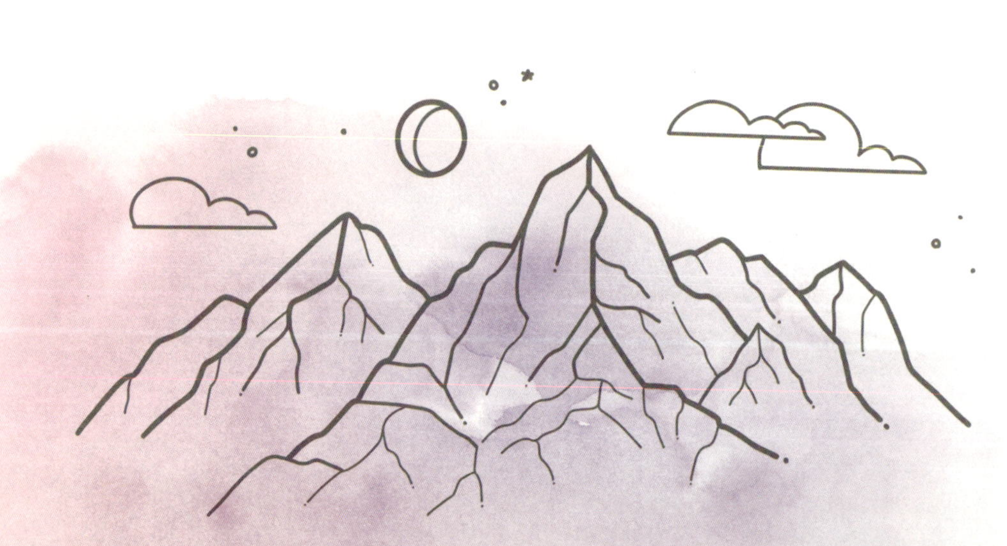

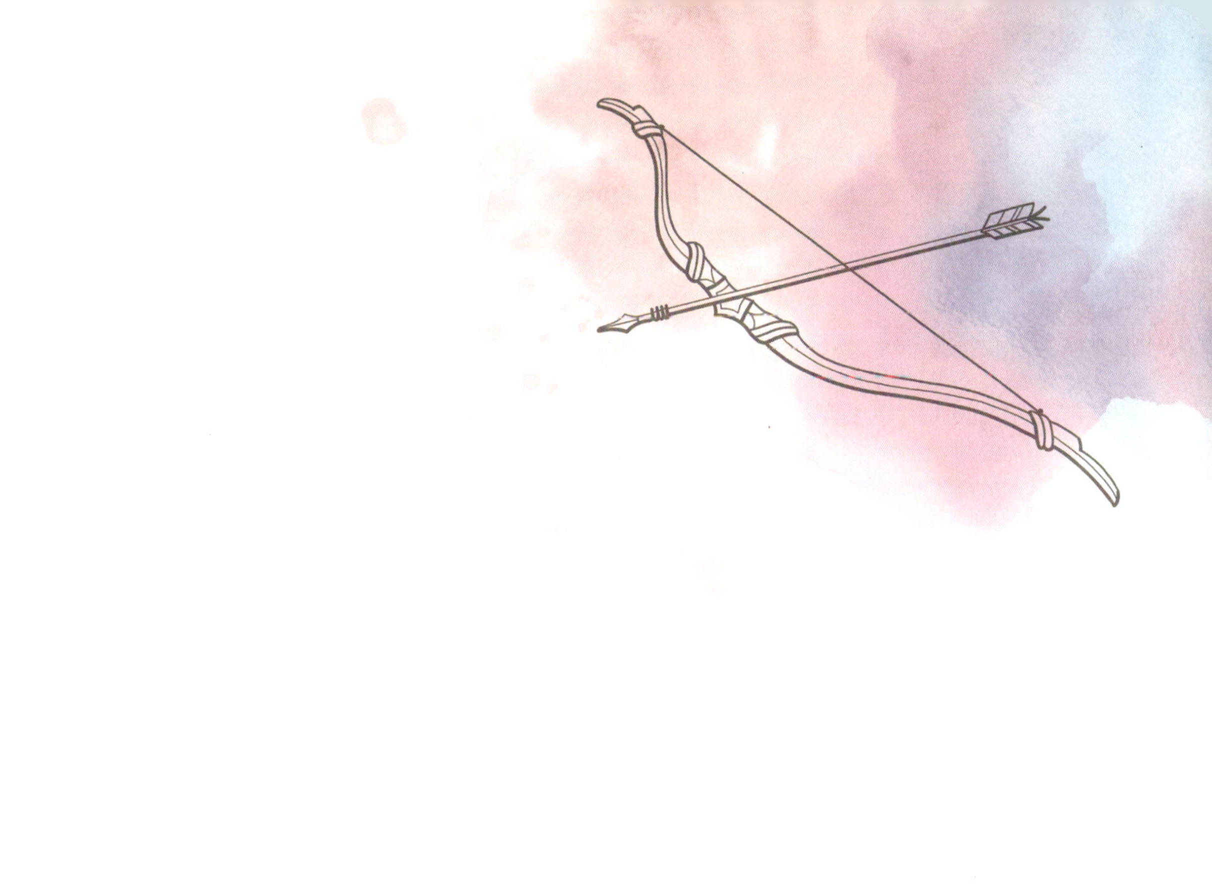

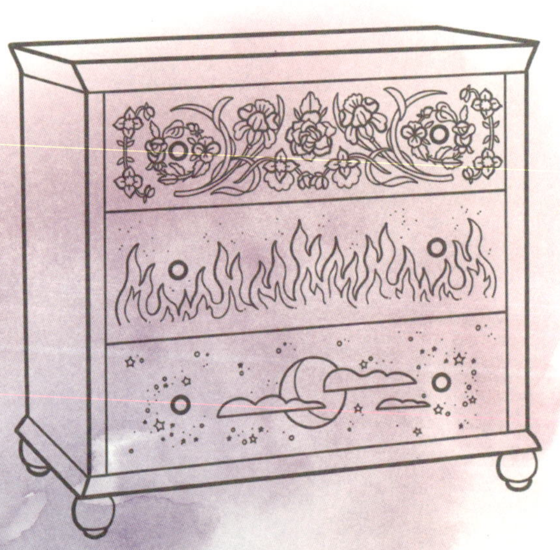

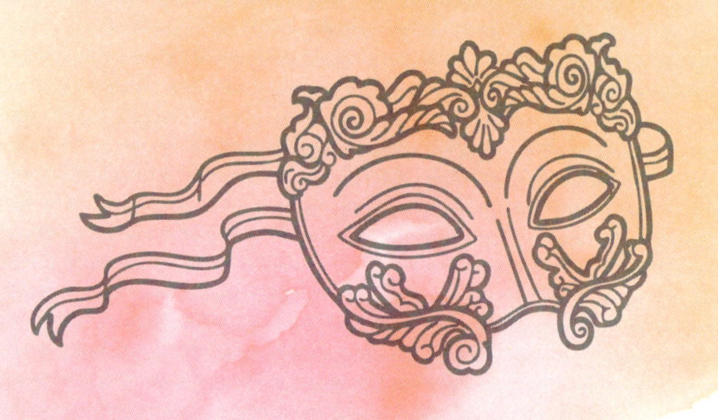

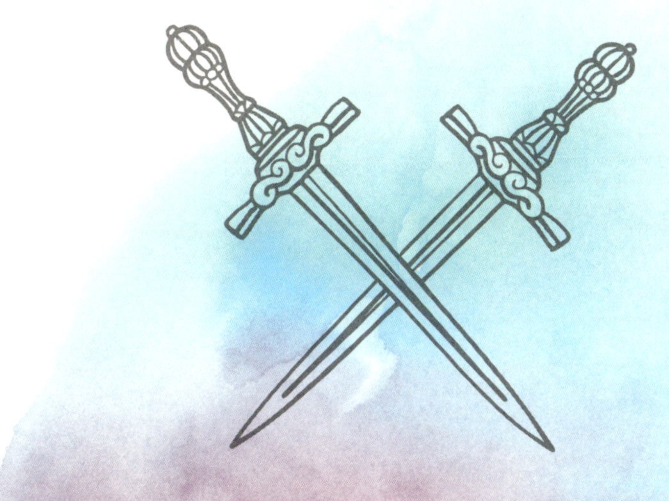

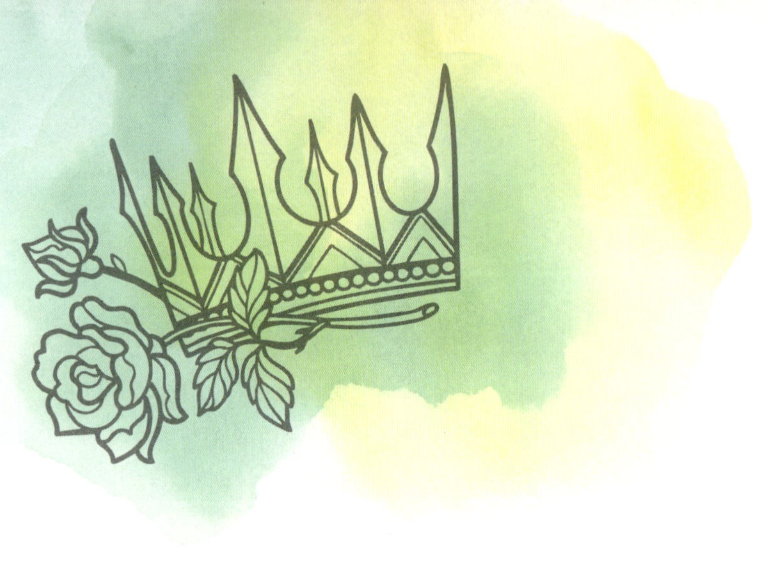

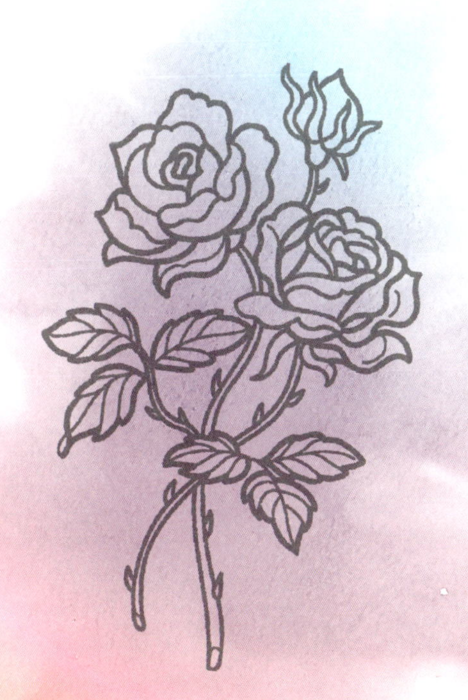

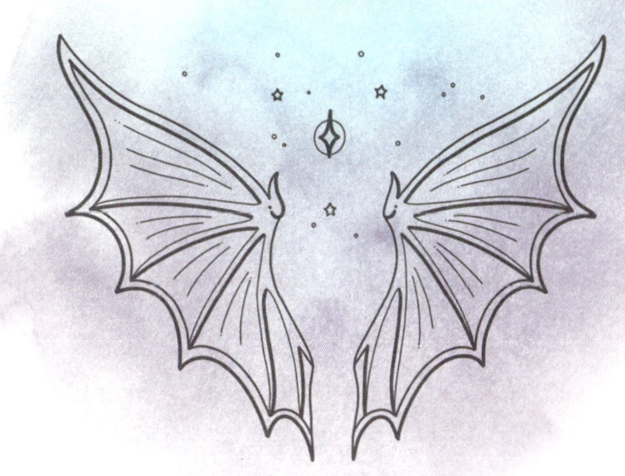

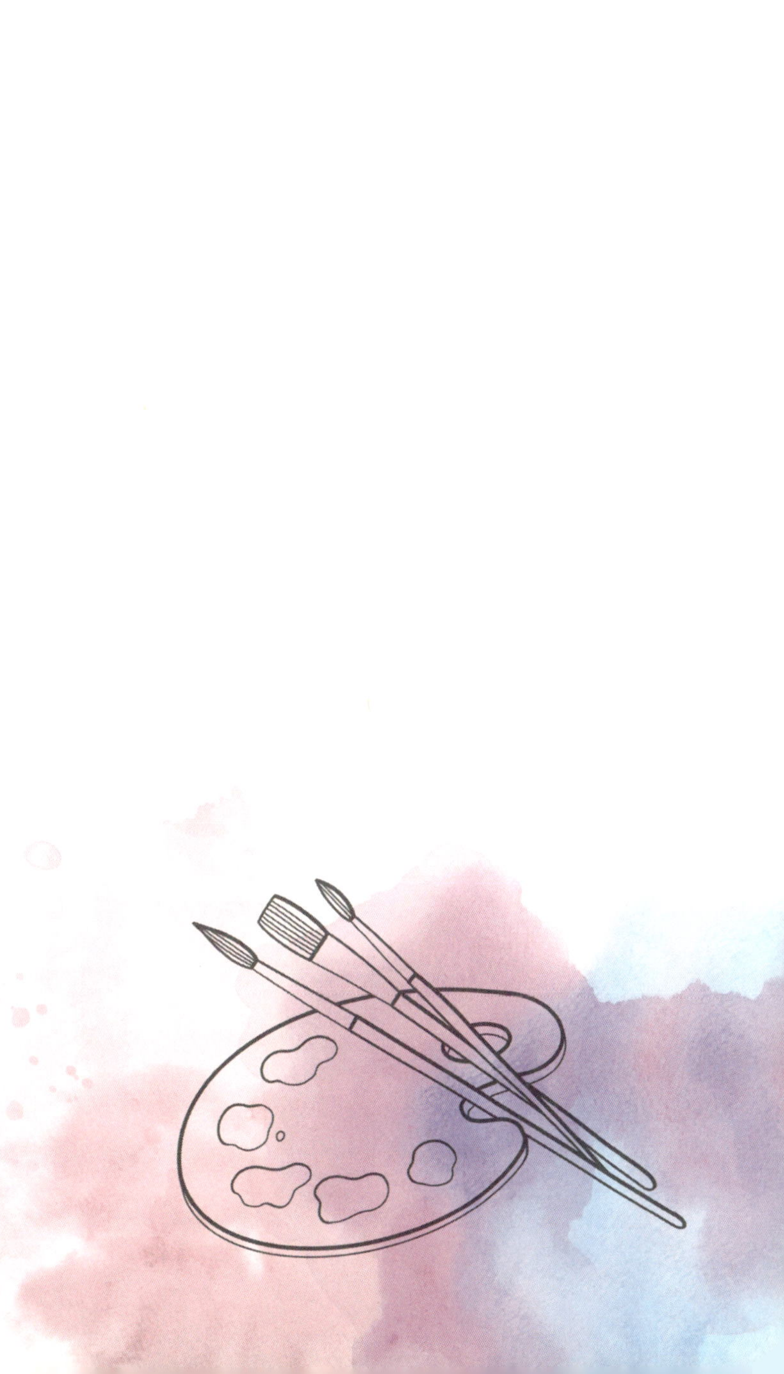

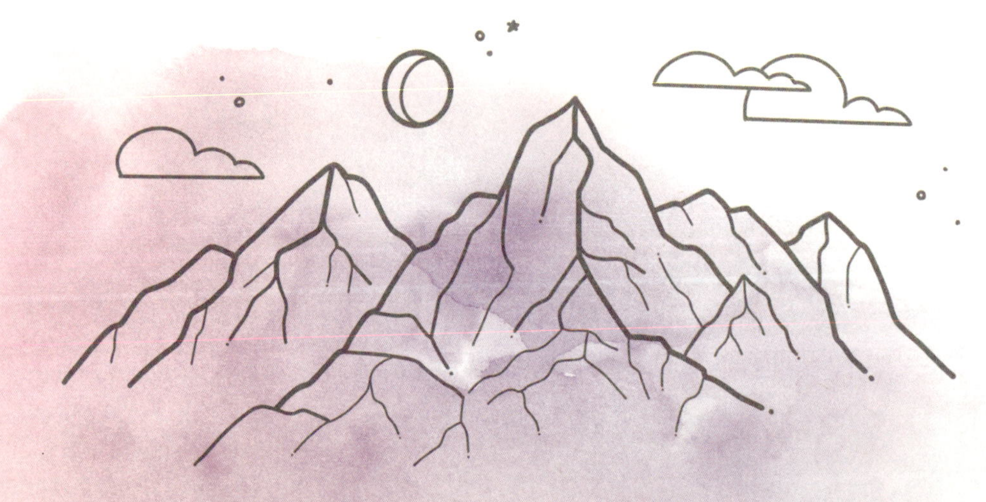

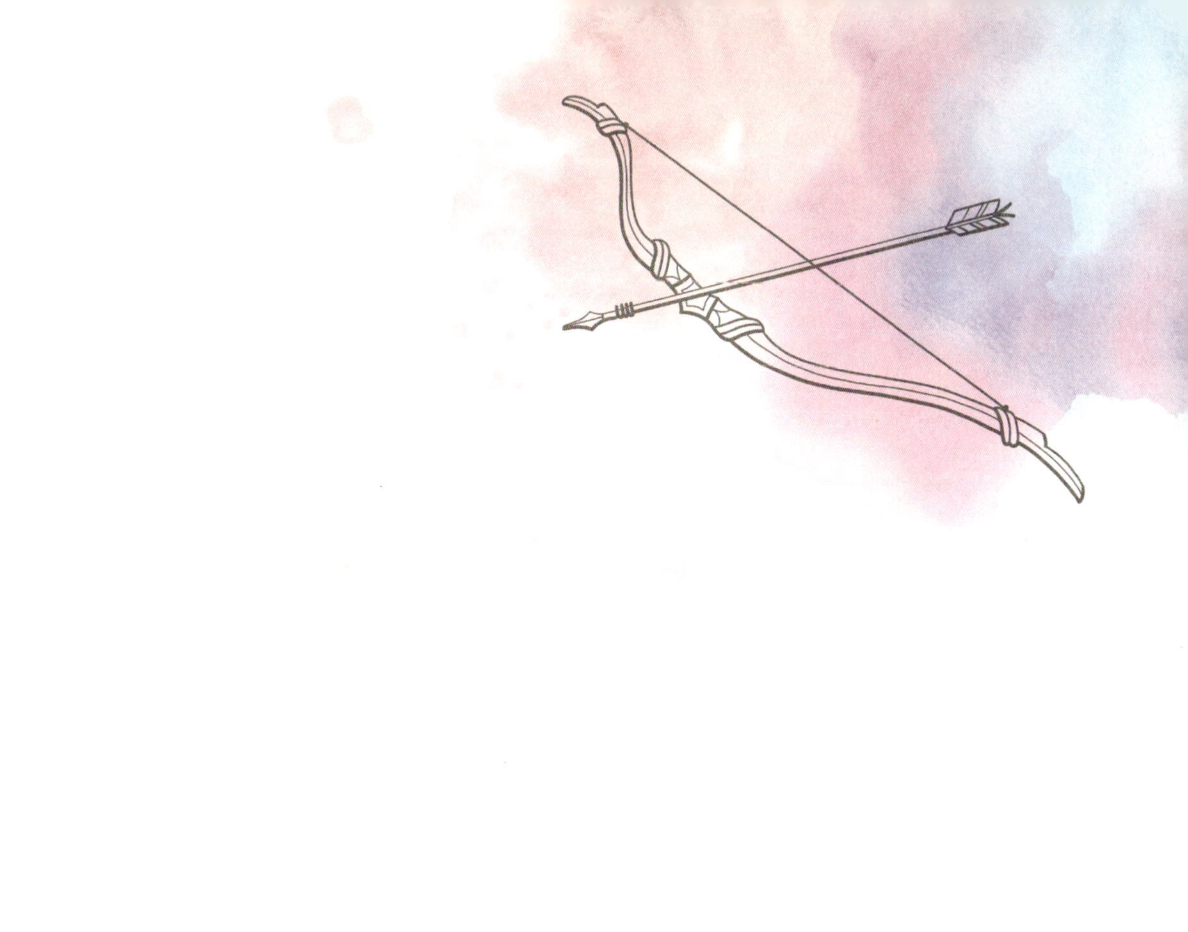

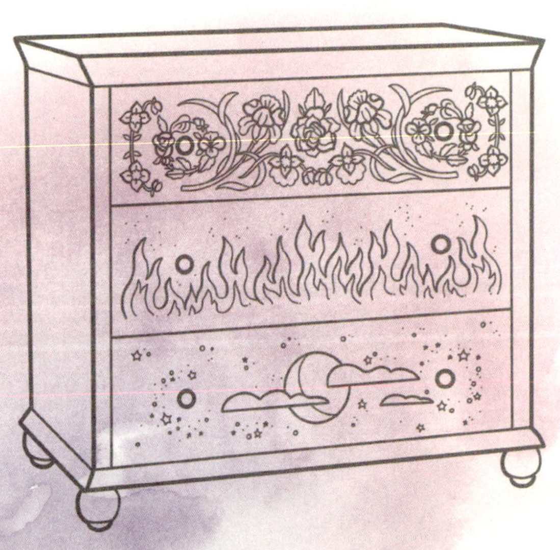

weldonowen

an imprint of Insight Editions
P.O. Box 3088
San Rafael, CA 94912
www.weldonowen.com

Illustrations © 2025 Weldon Owen International

Illustrations by Jill De Haan

All rights reserved. No part of this book may be reproduced
in any form without written permission from the publisher.

ISBN: 979-8-88674-302-9

Manufactured in China by Insight Editions
10 9 8 7 6 5 4 3 2 1

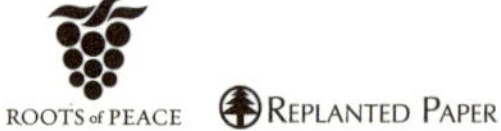

Insight Editions, in association with Roots of Peace, will plant two trees for each
tree used in the manufacturing of this book. Roots of Peace is an internationally
renowned humanitarian organization dedicated to eradicating land mines worldwide
and converting war-torn lands into productive farms and wildlife habitats. Roots of
Peace will plant two million fruit and nut trees in Afghanistan and provide farmers
there with the skills and support necessary for sustainable land use.